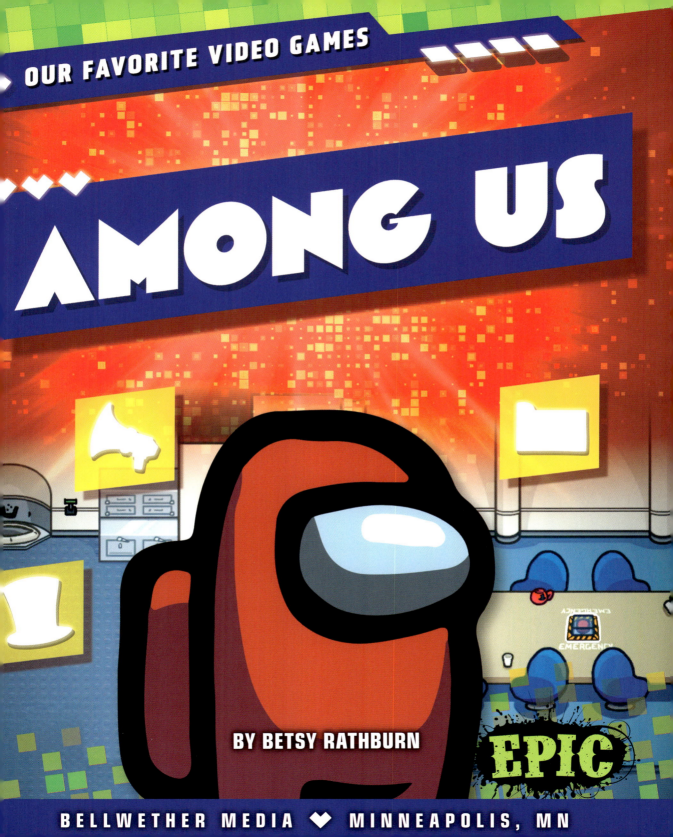

OUR FAVORITE VIDEO GAMES

AMONG US

BY BETSY RATHBURN

EPIC

BELLWETHER MEDIA ◆ MINNEAPOLIS, MN

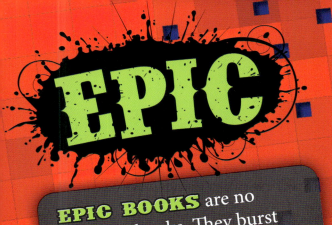

EPIC BOOKS are no ordinary books. They burst with intense action, high-speed heroics, and shadows of the unknown. Are you ready for an Epic adventure?

This is not an official *Among Us* book. It is not approved by or connected with Innersloth.

This edition first published in 2026 by Bellwether Media, Inc.

No part of this publication may be reproduced in whole or in part without written permission of the publisher. For information regarding permission, write to Bellwether Media, Inc., Attention: Permissions Department, 3500 American Blvd W, Suite 150, Bloomington, MN 55431.

Library of Congress Cataloging-in-Publication Data

Names: Rathburn, Betsy author
Title: Among us / Betsy Rathburn.
Description: Minneapolis, MN : Bellwether Media, Inc, 2026. | Series: Our favorite video games | Includes bibliographical references and index. | Audience: Ages 7-12 | Audience: Grades 4-6 | Summary: "Engaging images accompany information about the video game Among Us. The combination of high-interest subject matter and light text is intended for students in grades 2 through 7"-- Provided by publisher.
Identifiers: LCCN 2025003641 (print) | LCCN 2025003642 (ebook) | ISBN 9798893045048 (library binding) | ISBN 9798893047332 (paperback) | ISBN 9798893046427 (ebook)
Subjects: LCSH: Among us (Video game)--Juvenile literature.
Classification: LCC GV1469.37 .R367 2026 (print) | LCC GV1469.37 (ebook) | DDC 794.8--dc23/eng/20250313
LC record available at https://lccn.loc.gov/2025003641
LC ebook record available at https://lccn.loc.gov/2025003642

Text copyright © 2026 by Bellwether Media, Inc. EPIC and associated logos are trademarks and/or registered trademarks of Bellwether Media, Inc. Bellwether Media is a division of FlutterBee Education Group.

Editor: Christina Leaf   Designer: Gabriel Hilger

Printed in the United States of America, North Mankato, MN.

TABLE OF CONTENTS

WORKING TOGETHER	4
THE HISTORY OF AMONG US	10
AMONG US TODAY	18
AMONG US FANS	20
GLOSSARY	22
TO LEARN MORE	23
INDEX	24

WORKING TOGETHER

Players work to finish their tasks in *Among Us*. Suddenly, a meeting is called. The **impostor** has attacked!

The players vote to **eject** who they think the impostor is. They guess wrong. The impostor is still among them!

Among Us is an **online multiplayer game**. Crewmates do **minigames** to complete tasks. They win if they finish their tasks.

CREWMATES

MINIGAME

Impostors **sabotage** and attack crewmates. If they **eliminate** all crewmates, they win!

Players call meetings. Crewmates try to find all impostors. The impostors try to make others believe they are crewmates.

Everyone votes. If all impostors are voted out, the crewmates win!

Victory

THE HISTORY OF AMONG US

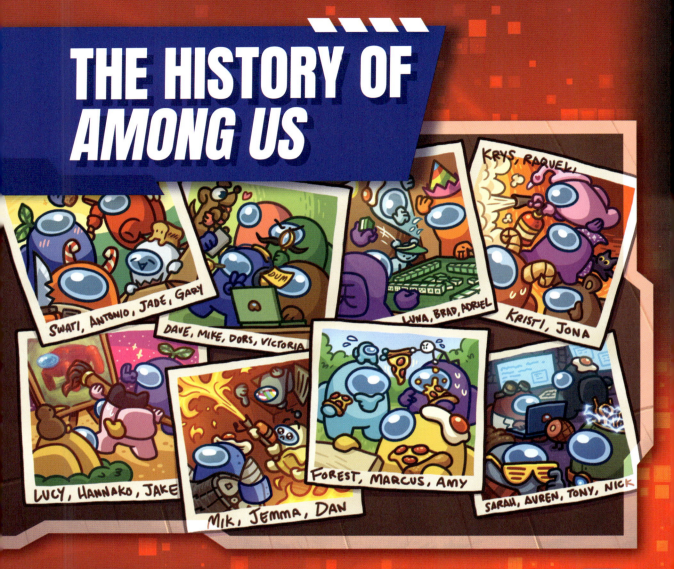

In 2017, a company called Innersloth began making *Among Us*. It was based on an idea by Marcus Bromander.

The game was released in 2018. But few people played it at first.

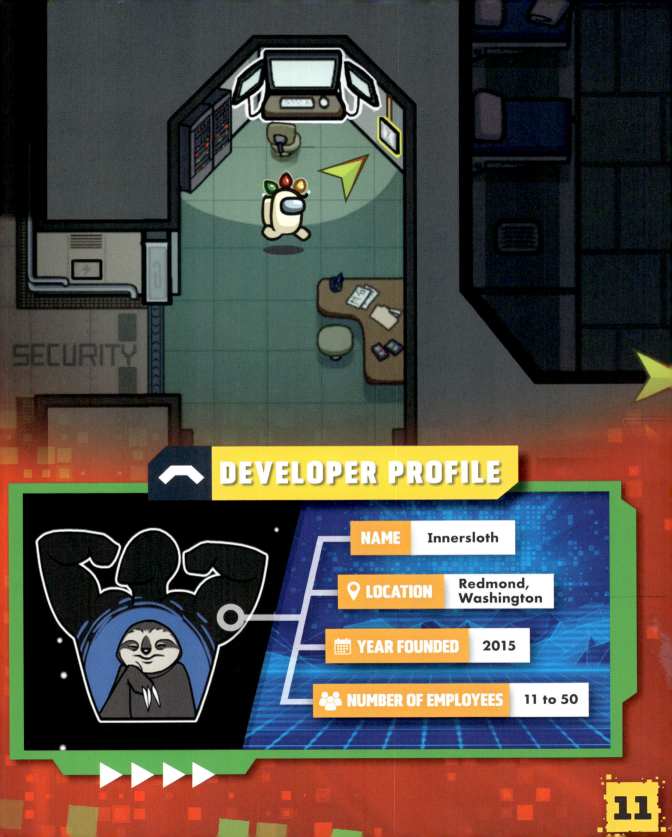

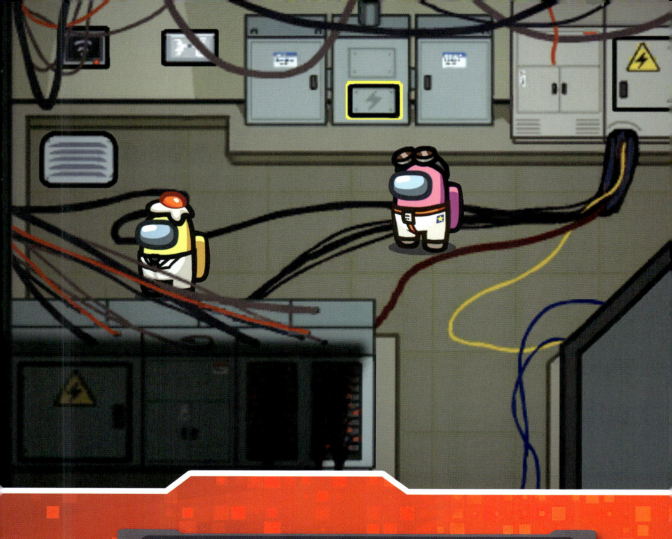

Popular **streamers** began playing *Among Us*. Their viewers started to play. The game slowly grew.

In 2020, **COVID-19** forced people to stay home. Many turned to video games. *Among Us* grew even more.

AMONG US TIMELINE

2018
Among Us is first released

2020
Among Us is released for the Nintendo Switch

March 2021
The Airship map is added to *Among Us*

December 2021
Among Us is released for PlayStation and Xbox consoles

2022
Among Us VR is released

In December 2020, the game came out for the Nintendo Switch. Its popularity exploded! In 2021, the Airship map was added. New roles were also added. Each role came with a new **ability**!

NINTENDO SWITCH

More New Roles

Three more new roles were added in 2024!

14

AMONG US ROLES

SHAPESHIFTER

ABILITY
take on the appearance of a crewmate

ENGINEER

ABILITY
use vents as a crewmate

NOISEMAKER

ABILITY
warn other crewmates when attacked

TRACKER

ABILITY
track other crewmates

GUARDIAN ANGEL

ABILITY
protect other crewmates

PHANTOM

ABILITY
turn invisible for a short period of time

SCIENTIST

ABILITY
see everyone's health at any point

15

FAN FAVORITE

Among Us won many awards. In 2021, it won a Kids' Choice Award for Favorite Video Game!

Among Us VR was released in 2022. Players use **virtual reality** headsets to play. Over 1 million copies were sold!

16

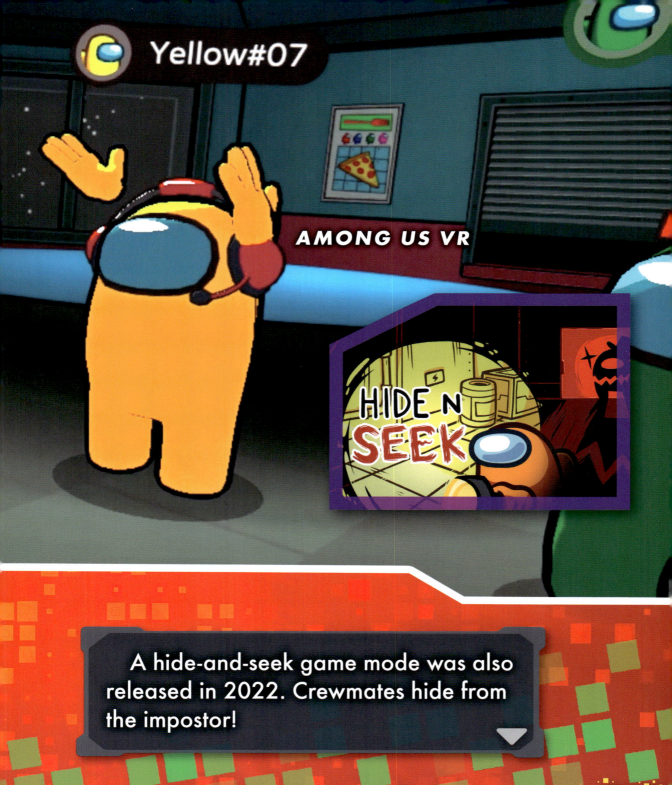

Yellow#07

AMONG US VR

A hide-and-seek game mode was also released in 2022. Crewmates hide from the impostor!

AMONG US TODAY

Tens of millions of people play *Among Us* each month. Gamers can play on computers, **consoles**, and **mobile devices**.

AMONG US PLAYERS

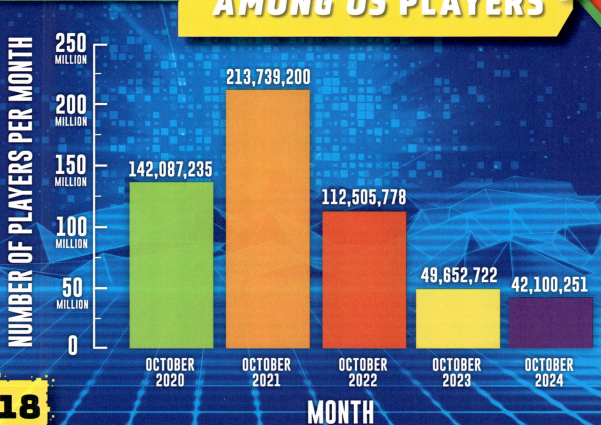

NUMBER OF PLAYERS PER MONTH

- October 2020: 142,087,235
- October 2021: 213,739,200
- October 2022: 112,505,778
- October 2023: 49,652,722
- October 2024: 42,100,251

MONTH

18

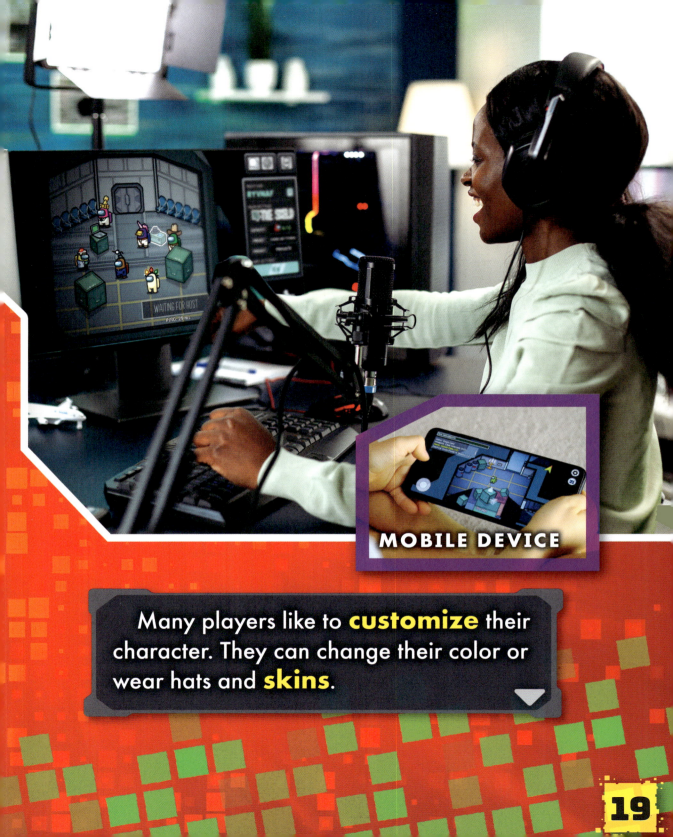

MOBILE DEVICE

Many players like to **customize** their character. They can change their color or wear hats and **skins**.

19

AMONG US FANS

Many fans enjoy making art of their characters. They draw their own hats and skins.

In 2023, Innersloth announced an *Among Us* TV show. The company has plenty more in store for *Among Us* fans!

AMONG US TV SHOW

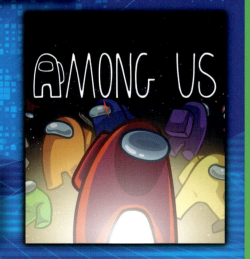

FIRST ANNOUNCED	June 2023
STUDIO	CBS Studios
STARRING	Elijah Wood, Randall Park, Yvette Nicole Brown, Ashley Johnson

GLOSSARY

ability—something someone is able to do

consoles—game systems that connect to TVs to play video games

COVID-19—a virus that led to shutdowns and millions of deaths around the world

customize—to change something to make it look or behave in a certain way

eject—to force someone or something out

eliminate—to remove or get rid of someone or something

impostor—a person who pretends to be someone or something that they are not

minigames—short games that are part of larger games

mobile devices—devices such as smartphones or tablets that can be used on the go

online multiplayer game—a game where two or more people play together online

sabotage—to intentionally stop or ruin something

skins—items that change the appearance of characters in a game

streamers—people who play for an online audience

virtual reality—related to computer technology that makes users feel like they are somewhere else

TO LEARN MORE

AT THE LIBRARY

Galanin, Dennis. *The Amazing World of Video Game Development.* Sanger, Calif.: Familius, 2022.

Gregory, Josh. *Starter Guide to Among Us.* Ann Arbor, Mich.: Cherry Lake Publishing, 2024.

Neuenfeldt, Elizabeth. *Video Games.* Minneapolis, Minn.: Bellwether Media, 2023.

ON THE WEB

Factsurfer.com gives you a safe, fun way to find more information.

1. Go to www.factsurfer.com.

2. Enter "Among Us" into the search box and click 🔍.

3. Select your book cover to see a list of related content.

INDEX

Airship map, 14
Among Us VR, 16, 17
awards, 16
Bromander, Marcus, 10
computers, 18
consoles, 14, 18
COVID-19, 12
crewmates, 6, 7, 8, 9, 17
fans, 20
hide-and-seek, 17
history, 10, 12, 13, 14,
    16, 17, 20
impostor, 4, 7, 8, 9, 17
Innersloth, 10, 11, 20
minigames, 6
mobile devices, 18, 19

online multiplayer game, 6
players, 4, 8, 10, 12, 16,
    18, 19
roles, 14, 15
sales, 16
streamers, 12
timeline, 13
TV show, 20

The images in this book are reproduced through the courtesy of: Samuelch50, front cover; Gabriel Hilger, pp. 3, 5, 6 (all), 7, 8 (all), 9, 11, 12, 13 (2018, March 2021), 14 (fact), 21; pbombaerta/ AdobeStock, p. 4; Innersloth, pp. 10, 11 (Innersloth logo), 16-17, 17, 20; canbedone, p. 13 (2020); Diego Thomazini, p. 13 (December 2021); PixieMe, p. 13 (2022); Vantage_DS, p. 14 (Nintendo Switch); Suzan Moore/ Alamy Stock Photo, p. 16 (fan favorite); DC Studio/ AdobeStock, p. 19; Ascannio/ Alamy Stock Photo, p. 19 (mobile device); Tigrushka, p. 23.